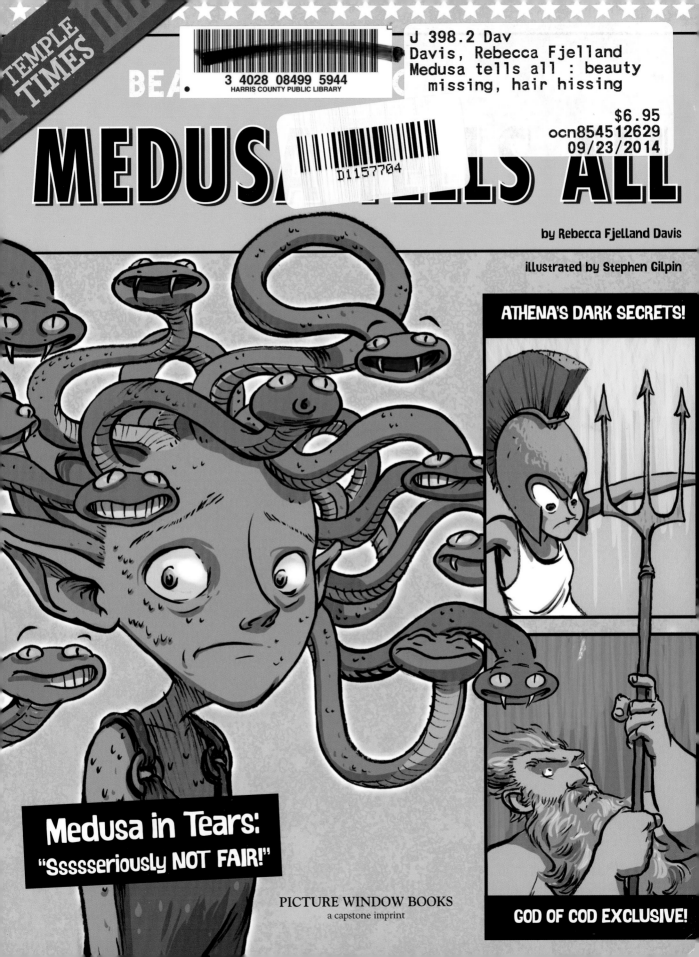

TEMPLE TIMES

BEA...

MEDUSA TELLS ALL

by Rebecca Fjelland Davis

illustrated by Stephen Gilpin

ATHENA'S DARK SECRETS!

Medusa in Tears:
"Ssssseriously NOT FAIR!"

PICTURE WINDOW BOOKS
a capstone imprint

GOD OF COD EXCLUSIVE!

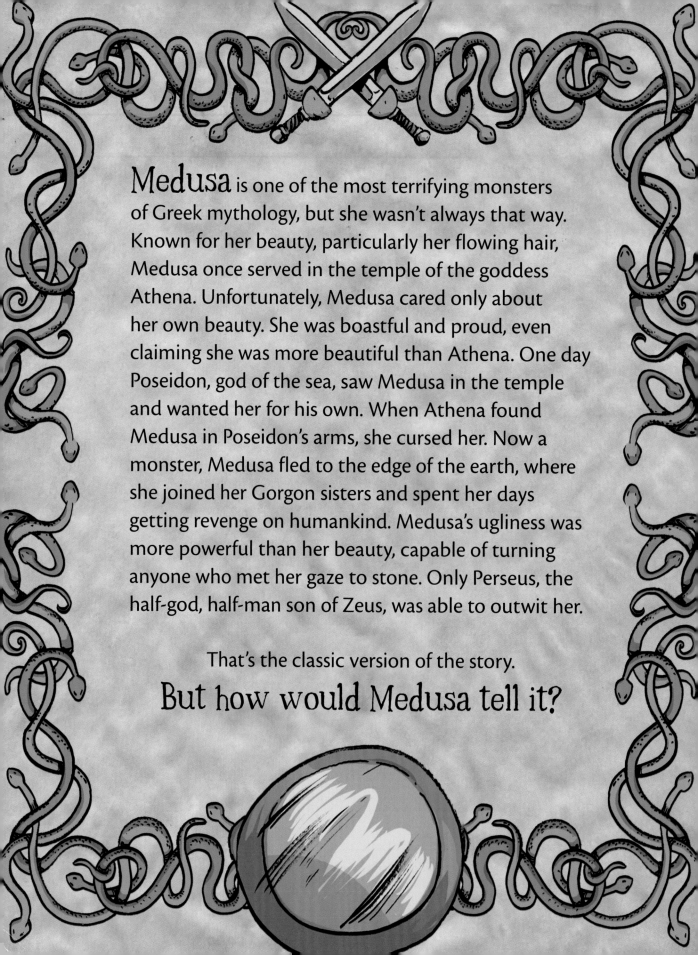

Medusa is one of the most terrifying monsters of Greek mythology, but she wasn't always that way. Known for her beauty, particularly her flowing hair, Medusa once served in the temple of the goddess Athena. Unfortunately, Medusa cared only about her own beauty. She was boastful and proud, even claiming she was more beautiful than Athena. One day Poseidon, god of the sea, saw Medusa in the temple and wanted her for his own. When Athena found Medusa in Poseidon's arms, she cursed her. Now a monster, Medusa fled to the edge of the earth, where she joined her Gorgon sisters and spent her days getting revenge on humankind. Medusa's ugliness was more powerful than her beauty, capable of turning anyone who met her gaze to stone. Only Perseus, the half-god, half-man son of Zeus, was able to outwit her.

That's the classic version of the story.

But how would Medusa tell it?

I am Medusa. You've seen my face before. It's supposed to be one of the scariest in the world. But let me tell you—it's *not* my fault I'm scary! It's all Athena's fault.

Everybody *loves* Athena. She's got the biggest, most beautiful, most famous temple in the world dedicated to her: the Parthenon in the city of Athens.

But Athena is a big BULLY! Want proof? Here's the real story.

You wouldn't know it now, but I was born beautiful. *Stunningly* beautiful. Everybody wants to be beautiful. There's nothing more important than beauty.

My sisters, the Gorgons, on the other hand, were born ugly. They live at the edge of the world so hardly anyone has to look at them, ever.

The trade-off is that my sisters are immortal. That means they'll live forever. Not me. I'm mortal, the opposite of immortal. But I'd rather be beautiful than live forever. Wouldn't you?

One day Athena noticed me. She thought I was beautiful, so she wanted me to serve in her temple. Me! What an honor!

I felt like the luckiest girl in the world.

I HAD NEVER BEEN SO WRONG.

Right away Athena was jealous of me. She wanted me in the temple because I was beautiful. But as soon as I got there, she was jealous of how the men looked at *me* instead of her.

I couldn't help it if men turned and stared at my long, flowing hair. OK, maybe I swished it on purpose when I walked, when I knew someone was looking. But the problem wasn't me. It was Athena.

I guess it's dangerous to be more beautiful than a goddess.

One day Poseidon came into the temple. You can't miss it when Poseidon, the god of the sea, arrives. He rolls in with great curling waves and the rush of high tide. And if you aren't careful, he'll knock you right off your feet.

Poseidon and Athena aren't the best of friends. Actually, they hate each other. Ages ago they competed to rule over Athens, and Athena won—that's why the city is called Athens.

"And who might you be?" Poseidon asked me with a crash of waves.

"Medusa," I said. "I am Medusa."

"Medusa, is it?" Poseidon smiled a smile like the ocean, full of sandy beaches and polished sea glass.

I liked his smile. I liked him.

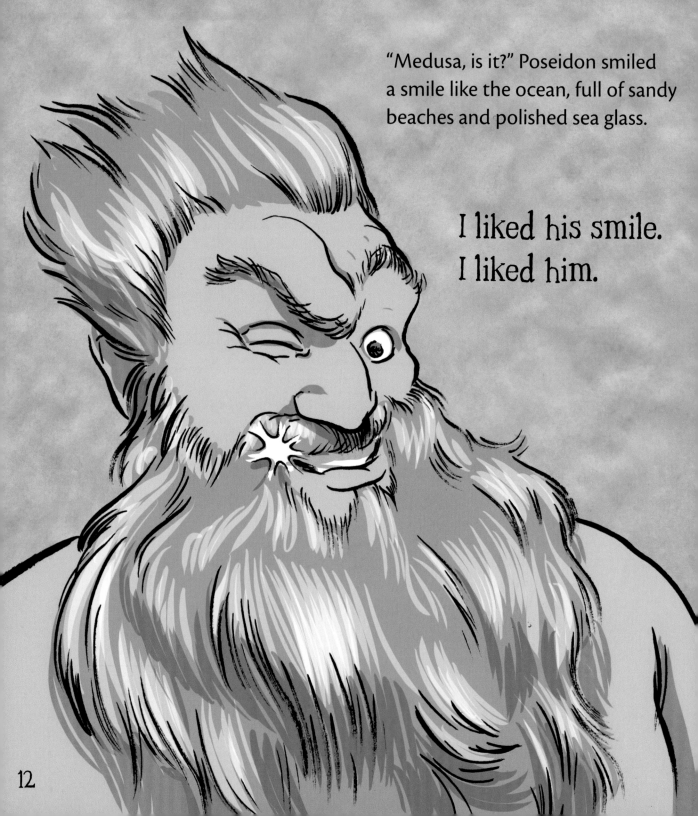

"Athena, my dear," Poseidon bellowed, "why have you kept the most beautiful girl in the world hidden from me in your temple all this time?"

That's when Poseidon's tide knocked me off my feet. I really didn't mind at first. But then I couldn't get up. I got nervous.

Waves of Poseidon's laughter slammed against the walls of the temple.

"Athena!" I cried out. "Help me!" But Athena glared at me, turned on her heel, and disappeared.

I was alone with Poseidon. The force of the seawater was strong, too strong, and I could not get up, no matter how hard I tried. I felt as if I were drowning.

Finally Poseidon left. The temple quieted. I lay limp on the floor, drenched in seawater, seaweed in my hair.

As echoes of Poseidon's laughter died away, Athena returned. I should've been furious with her for leaving me to fend for myself. But I wasn't. Truth be told, I was so shaken up that it was a relief to see a familiar face.

I raised my hand for Athena to help me up, but she pointed at the door.

16

I told you she's a bully.

"Please!" I begged. "Don't send me away. It's not my fault!"

"CURSES!" Athena screamed. "Curses upon your beauty, Medusa!"

Her curse words swirled around me. I felt my skin stretching and my hair getting heavy ... and moving. My hair, my beautiful hair, became writhing, poisonous snakes! They hissed and slithered on my shoulders.

"No!" I screamed. I fell at Athena's feet. "No! Please!"

"Be gone!" she commanded.

And so I went, with only my snakes as companions.

Yes, at the time, I was horrified when my hair came to life. But I have to take a moment here to say I don't understand all the fuss. Who cares about a few little poisonous snakes anyway? They never bite anyone! Ever!

OK, the truth is that nobody ever gets close enough to me for my snakes to *bite*. Everyone is too—shall we say—*petrified*.

Back to my story.

Outside the temple I saw a man. Surely he would feel sorry for me. He would see my true beauty, and I'd tell him what a bully Athena was.

He looked at me, as men always did, and I shook my head so my hair would shimmer. But instead the snakes raised their heads and hissed.

The man froze with fear. He couldn't move. Would you believe he *turned to stone*? I was used to my beauty stopping men in their tracks, but this was ridiculous.

From then on, everywhere I went, people looked upon my face and turned to stone. At the market ... the chariot races ... the springs ...

Can you see why this is all Athena's fault?

Some time later a "hero" came to town. His name was Perseus. He was half-god and half-man. His job was to take something from me: MY HEAD. And who do you think was helping him? Athena, of course. She couldn't be satisfied that she made me into a monster. No, she wanted to finish me off.

Athena had given Perseus her shield. It was as shiny as a mirror so he could see me without looking directly at me. Stygian nymphs had loaned Perseus the cap of invisibility so I couldn't see him coming. And Hermes, the messenger god, had given Perseus winged sandals so he could fly to me without making a sound. Everyone was against me.

It wasn't fair!

Well, anyway, Perseus held up Athena's
shield, and the last thing I saw was his sword
swinging toward my neck.

So Perseus killed me. I am dead.

But let me tell you this. Even though the big bully
Athena helped Perseus kill me, I will live forever.

You can still see my face in Athena's shield.
All you have to do is look.

I dare you.

Talk It Out ★ ★ ★ ★ ★ ★ ★ ★ ★ ★ ★ ★ ★ ★ ★ ★ ★ ★

Most classic versions of the Medusa myth are told by an invisible narrator who takes Perseus' side. This version is told by Medusa, from her point of view. If Athena told the story, what details might she tell differently? What if Poseidon told the story from his point of view?

Athena refused to help Medusa after Poseidon's attack. Describe how the rest of the story might have changed if she had helped.

Medusa claims that everything—Poseidon's actions, Medusa's snake hair and scaly skin, people turned into stone—was Athena's fault. Do you believe her? Why or why not? Give examples to support your answer.

Medusa's sisters are immortal, but Medusa is not. Describe what life would be like if you were immortal but your friends and family were not, or vice versa. Discuss the pros and cons of immortality.

Read More

Gunderson, Jessica. *Medusa's Stony Stare: A Retelling.* Greek Myths. Mankato, Minn.: Picture Window Books, 2012.

Jeffrey, Gary. *Perseus Slays the Gorgon Medusa.* Graphic Mythical Heroes. New York: Gareth Stevens Pub., 2013.

Lock, Deborah. *Greek Myths.* DK Readers. 3, Reading Alone. New York: DK, 2008.

Storrie, Paul D. *Perseus: The Hunt for Medusa's Head: A Greek Myth.* Graphic Myths and Legends. Minneapolis: Graphic Universe, 2008.

Glossary

Athens—the capital city of Greece

Gorgon—one of three monstrous creatures with hair of living snakes

immortal—capable of living forever and never dying

mortal—human, referring to a being who will eventually die

mythology—old or ancient stories told again and again that help connect people with their past

narrator—a person who tells a story

Parthenon—the temple of Athena, on the Acropolis (the high point of the city) in Athens

point of view—a way of looking at something

Stygian nymph—a girl-like creature from Hades, the underground land of the dead in Greek mythology

version—an account of something from a certain point of view

Thanks to our advisers for their expertise, research, and advice:

Susan C. Shelmerdine, PhD, Professor of Classical Studies
University of North Carolina, Greensboro

Terry Flaherty, PhD, Professor of English
Minnesota State University, Mankato

Editor: Jill Kalz
Designer: Lori Bye
Art Director: Nathan Gassman
Production Specialist: Danielle Ceminsky
The illustrations in this book were created digitally.

Picture Window Books are published by Capstone,
1710 Roe Crest Drive, North Mankato, Minnesota 56003
www.capstonepub.com

Library of Congress Cataloging-in-Publication Data
Davis, Rebecca Fjelland.
  Medusa tells all : beauty missing, hair hissing / by Rebecca Fjelland Davis ;
illustrated by Stephen Gilpin.
     pages cm.—(The other side of the myth)
  Summary: "Introduces the concept of point of view through Medusa's retelling
of the classic Greek myth 'Medusa'"—Provided by publisher.
  ISBN 978-1-4795-2185-2 (library binding)
  ISBN 978-1-4795-2942-1 (paperback)
  ISBN 978-1-4795-2960-5 (paper over board)
  ISBN 978-1-4795-3321-3 (ebook PDF)
1. Medusa (Greek mythology)—Juvenile literature. I. Gilpin, Stephen, illustrator.
II. Title.
  BL820.M38D38 2014
  202'.114—dc23
                                        2013027678

photo credit: Steve Deger

About the Author

Rebecca Fjelland Davis lives near Good Thunder,
Minnesota. Her young adult novels include *Chasing
AllieCat* (Flux), a Junior Library Guild Selection; and
Jake Riley: Irreparably Damaged (HarperCollins),
a BCCB Blue Ribbon Fiction Book. Rebecca has
also written a number of nonfiction books for
children. An instructor at South Central College
(North Mankato, Minn.), she teaches English and
Humanities, and loves Greek mythology!

Look for all the books in the series:

CYCLOPS TELLS ALL: THE WAY EYE SEE IT
MEDEA TELLS ALL: A MAD, MAGICAL LOVE
MEDUSA TELLS ALL: BEAUTY MISSING, HAIR HISSING
PANDORA TELLS ALL: NOT THE CURIOUS KIND

Printed in the United States of America in Brainerd, Minnesota.
092013   007770BANGS14